D0487454

This book is to be returned on or before

Daniel Stewart's and Melville College

* 0 0 0 0 9 3 3 0 *

EXPLORING THE SOLAR SYSTEM

SATURN

GILES SPARROW

Heinemann
LIBRARY

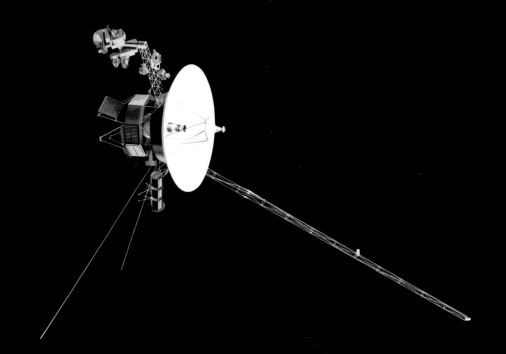

SATURN

Published by Heinemann Library,
a division of Reed Educational & Professional Publishing,
Halley Court, Jordan Hill,
Oxford OX2 8EJ, UK
Visit our website at www.heinemann.co.uk/library

All rights reserved. No part of this publication may be reproduced or
transmitted in any form or by any means, electronic or mechanical,
including photocopying, recording, taping, or any information storage and
retrieval system, without permission in writing from the publisher.

Produced by Brown Partworks
Project Editor: Ben Morgan
Deputy Editor: Sally McFall
Managing Editor: Anne O'Daly
Designer: Steve Wilson
Illustrator: Mark Walker
Picture Researcher: Helen Simm
Consultant: Peter Bond

© 2001 Brown Partworks Limited

Printed in Singapore

ISBN 0 431 12264 4 (hardback)   *ISBN 0 431 12273 3 (paperback)*
06 05 04 03 02 01   *06 05 04 03 02 01*
10 9 8 7 6 5 4 3 2 1   *10 9 8 7 6 5 4 3 2 1*

British Library Cataloguing in Publication Data

Sparrow, Giles
  Saturn. – (Exploring the solar system)
  1.Saturn (Planet) – Juvenile literature
  I.Title
  523.4'6

BELOW: *The planets of the Solar System, shown in order from the Sun:*
Mercury, Venus, Earth, Mars, Jupiter, Saturn, Uranus, Neptune, Pluto.

CONTENTS

*Some words are shown in bold, **like this**.*
You can find out what they mean by looking in the glossary.

Where is Saturn?

Saturn, famous for its beautiful **rings**, lies far out in the Solar System. It is the most distant planet we can see clearly with the naked eye. For centuries Saturn was the furthest known planet, until the invention of the telescope led to the discovery of Uranus, Neptune and tiny Pluto.

Saturn is a **gas giant** – one of the huge planets made of gas that inhabit the outer Solar System. This second largest planet, only slightly smaller than Jupiter, could swallow Earth nearly 1000 times over.

Like all the planets, Saturn moves around the Sun along a path called an **orbit**. The time it takes to complete one orbit is the length of its year. Because Saturn is nearly ten times further from the Sun than Earth, its orbit is much longer and its year is about 30 Earth years. Saturn's orbit is roughly circular, so it keeps a fairly steady distance from the Sun. But its distance from Earth changes constantly, depending on the positions of both planets in their orbits. Saturn is closest to us when it lines up with Earth on the same side of the Sun, which happens once every fifteen years.

Getting to Saturn

The time it takes to reach Saturn depends on your method of transport, and on the positions of Earth and Saturn in their orbits when you set off.

Distance from Earth to Saturn
Closest   **1.28 billion km**
              (793 million miles)
Furthest   **1.58 billion km**
              (979 million miles)

**By car at 117 km per hour
(70 miles per hour)**
Closest   **1292 years**
Furthest   **1595 years**

**By rocket at 11 km per second
(7 miles per second)**
Closest   **3 years 7 months**
Furthest   **4 years 5 months**

Time for radio signals to reach Saturn (at the speed of light)
Closest   **1 hour 11 minutes**
Furthest   **1 hour 28 minutes**

Distance from the Sun

The diagram shows how far the planets are from the Sun. Many million kilometres from Earth, Saturn is one of the outer planets, along with Jupiter, Uranus, Neptune and Pluto.

Sun   Mercury   Venus   Earth   Mars   Jupiter   Saturn

0   1000 (621)   2000 (1243)

Distance in millions of kilometres (millions of miles)

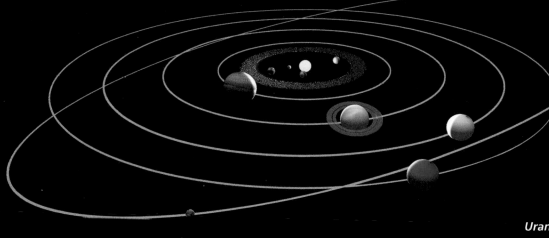

LEFT: *Saturn is the sixth planet from the Sun, after Mercury, Venus, Earth, Mars and Jupiter. Only three planets lie beyond it: Uranus, Neptune and Pluto.*

Saturn is at its furthest when Earth and Saturn line up on opposite sides of the Sun.

Imagine you're going to join a **mission** to Saturn. The trip there and back will last about twenty years, so you'll need to keep busy to avoid getting bored. In the future astronauts may be able to spend long space journeys asleep. Chemicals and extreme cold could preserve them in 'suspended animation', a state like hibernation. Unfortunately, scientists don't yet know how to do this.

As you leave Earth, your spaceship heads towards our neighbouring planet, Venus. You will fly close enough to Venus to get caught by its **gravity**, which will give the ship a tremendous boost of speed as it swings around the planet. This slingshot effect is often used by **space probes** to pick up speed. You will have to pass several planets this way to gain enough speed to reach Saturn.

Size compared to Earth

Earth's diameter:
12,756 km (7926 miles)

Saturn's diameter:
120,536 km (74,867 miles)

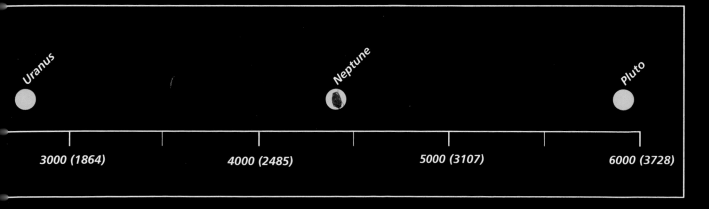

Uranus

Neptune

Pluto

3000 (1864)   4000 (2485)   5000 (3107)   6000 (3728)

From Earth, Saturn looks like a large yellow star. With good binoculars or a small telescope, it's just possible to make out the **rings**, which give the planet an odd, lumpy shape. By the time your ship reaches Jupiter, where another slingshot gives you a boost of speed, you can see Saturn's lumpy shape clearly with the naked eye.

ABOVE: *Your first view of Saturn will look similar to this picture of the planet taken from Earth through a large telescope. You should just be able to make out some faint stripes on Saturn, and its glowing rings, broken by a large, dark gap known as the Cassini division. In this image the star 28 Sagittarii (right) can be seen shining through the gap.*

From your angle of approach the rings look like enormous handles. From Earth the angle of the rings changes throughout Saturn's **orbit** – every fifteen years they are as wide and obvious as they are now, but in between they get narrower and narrower, almost vanishing for a few months when they are edge-on.

Compared to the rings, Saturn itself seems boring. It is a bright, creamy-white ball with faint horizontal stripes. The planet has cast a wide shadow over the rings, and the rings have cast another shadow on Saturn's face. You notice Saturn isn't a perfect circle – it looks squashed, as though the **poles** are too flat and the **equator** too wide.

You also see several bright points of light close to Saturn. These are just a few of the planet's huge family of moons.

BELOW: *Because the journey to Saturn will take about twenty years, you will need a very big spaceship to carry enough supplies – like the one in this artist's impression.*

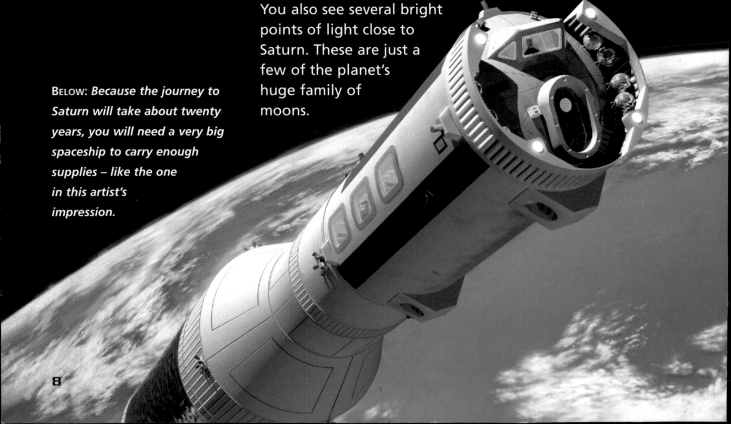

Getting closer

Finally you reach Saturn and see the planet in all its glory, the magnificent rings stretching tens of thousands of miles into space. Unlike the sooty rings around Jupiter, Saturn's rings are dazzlingly bright. In places they are broken by dark gaps, the widest of which is known as the Cassini division. As you get closer you see ever more gaps, and eventually you realize that there are actually thousands of separate rings around Saturn. Together they look like the grooves on an old-fashioned vinyl record.

Now you can see details on Saturn's face. The faint stripes you saw earlier are clear as broad bands of colour wrapping around the planet, rather like Jupiter's stripes. There are also several white blobs, including a large one close to the equator. But you can't see any land – Saturn is just a sea of clouds. By measuring the time that cloud features take to go around the planet, you can time Saturn's **rotation**. It turns out to be just 10 hours 14 minutes. Saturn is spinning so rapidly that the fastest moving areas, near the equator, are bulging out and giving the planet its squashed shape.

LEFT: *Saturn casts a shadow over its rings in this photograph taken by the* Voyager 1 *space probe*.

BELOW: **Voyager 2** *took this enhanced-colour picture of Saturn. The black dot on the lower half of the planet, below the rings, is the shadow of one of Saturn's moons.*

The rings

Your approach to Saturn takes you very close to the **rings**, giving you a really good look at them. From close up the rings look solid, but this is just an illusion. They can't be solid because Saturn's **gravity** would slowly tear apart any large object orb___ so close to the planet. Also, although the rings look mostly perfect, you can see gaps that radiate outwards from Saturn like spokes in a wheel, crossing several rings at once. Using coloured filters, your ship's cameras can discover what chemicals the rings are made of by analysing the light they reflect. It turns out the rings are mostly made of ice, which explains why they reflect light so brilliantly.

You steer the ship on a course that will pass the outer edge of the rings. As you watch, the rings get narrower and narrower, until they look paper thin. You're about to swoop past them when you realize, to your horror, that you've misjudged where the rings end. The region of space ahead of the ship is glowing slightly – there must be a very faint outer ring, and you're heading straight into it!

Saturn's rings are mostly ice, but other chemicals are present too. This photo from the Voyager 2 *probe shows chemical variations as different colours.*

Vanishing rings

Normally we see Saturn with its rings tilted, but once every fifteen years we see them edge-on. When this happens the rings almost vanish because they are so thin. These pictures from the Hubble Space Telescope show the rings edge-on and slightly tilted. Titan, Saturn's largest moon, appears in the left of the top image.

Bracing yourself, you watch as the main rings closer to Saturn get so narrow that they are just a straight line across the sky. You are now in the ring plane, and the ship is shaking and rattling as though it's going through a hailstorm. Then, in an instant, you're through.

The faint outer ring that you just crossed was only a few kilometres thick and was almost invisible, yet it extends into space an incredible distance – nearly six times further than Saturn's main rings. That gives Saturn and its rings a total diameter of about 1 million kilometres (600,000 miles) – about 75 times the width of Earth!

Once your ship is in a stable **orbit** around Saturn, you put on your spacesuit and take a **spacewalk** outside to inspect the ship for signs of damage. The ship is pitted with small dents, but fortunately the heavy shielding stood up to the bombardment. One of your sample scoops has collected some of the material from the outer ring – tiny fragments of dusty ice like specks of grit.

Saturn's rings look solid, even from nearby, but they are actually made of billions of chunks of ice orbiting Saturn together. This artist's impression shows the Cassini probe passing Saturn.

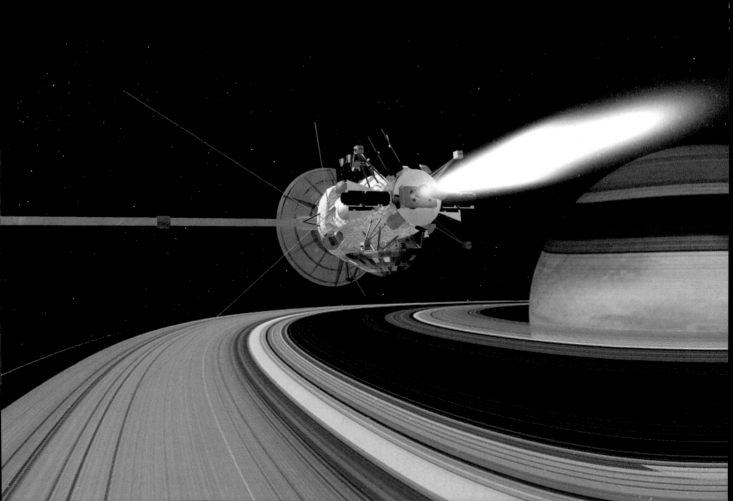

A world without a surface

Safely in **orbit** above Saturn, it's time to take a look at the planet itself. You're now close enough to see that the bands of clouds are swirling with just as much activity as Jupiter. The big difference is that while Jupiter's clouds are a colourful mixture of red, brown and blue, Saturn's are pale and muted. Saturn's clouds seem to come only in different shades of cream.

The clouds are not just a thin blanket over a mainly solid planet, like the clouds of Earth and Venus. Instead, Saturn is gas nearly all the way through, with just a small solid **core** at the centre. The cloud bands move around the planet at different rates, depending on their distance from the **equator**. As you watch over several hours, you can see that the clouds closest to the equator are moving slightly faster.

Saturn's seasons

Because Saturn spins on a tilt, it has seasons. Summer happens in the part of Saturn that is tilted towards the Sun, and winter happens in the part that is tilted away. Saturn's seasons are far longer than those of Earth. Because Saturn's year lasts about 30 Earth years, summer on the planet lasts about 8 Earth years.

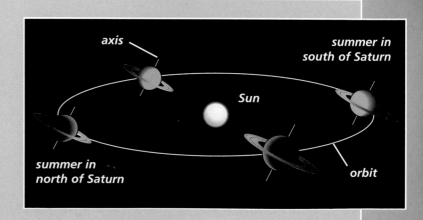

RIGHT: *The bands of clouds around Saturn can be hard to see, but this false-colour image from the* Voyager 2 *space probe shows them in great detail. Saturn's clouds are blown into swirling patterns by high winds, just like the clouds of Jupiter.*

It's hard to get an idea of scale from orbit, but Saturn is an enormous planet, with a diameter of about 121,000 kilometres (75,000 miles) across the equator. That makes Saturn nine times wider than Earth, but slightly smaller than Jupiter, the largest planet. From **pole** to pole, however, Saturn is only about 109,000 kilometres (68,000 miles) tall, making it the most squashed planet in the Solar System.

Like Earth, Saturn spins on a tilted **axis**, and this gives it different seasons as it orbits the Sun. When the **north pole** is tilted towards the Sun, it is summer in the northern **hemisphere** and winter in the southern hemisphere. You've arrived at the start of the northern summer and are just in time for one of Saturn's most spectacular, and least understood, events.

A huge storm has broken out north of the equator and is spreading around the planet as you watch. Like a thundercloud on Earth, the storm is caused by warm air rushing upwards. However, this storm is not just bigger than a storm on Earth, it is bigger than Earth itself! The storm looks white because icy crystals are forming in its freezing upper reaches. Ferocious winds of around 1600 kilometres per hour (1000 miles per hour) have blown into one side of the storm, giving it an arrow shape. As you watch, the winds blow huge masses of white clouds off the storm and send them hurtling across the planet, stirring up Saturn's stripes.

A colossal storm on Saturn shows up as a pale arrow shape in this picture from the Hubble Space Telescope.

Saturn's atmosphere

This artist's impression shows a parachute slowing down your probe as it plunges into Saturn's atmosphere.

Because Saturn has no solid surface, you can't land on the planet to explore. Instead, you decide to send down a **space probe** to study Saturn's **atmosphere**. This will give you some idea of what the cloud layers are made of, and what lies beneath them.

As the probe drops towards Saturn it starts sending back data. Its first discovery is that Saturn is surrounded by a strong **magnetic field** and a region of deadly **radiation**. The radiation is caused by the **solar wind**, a stream of electrically charged **particles** that pour constantly out of the Sun and rush through space at millions of kilometres an hour. Saturn's magnetic field traps particles from the solar wind and concentrates them, causing the deadly radiation.

The next discovery is a big surprise. Although Saturn is much bigger and heavier than Earth, its **gravity** is actually slightly weaker than gravity on the surface of Earth. This means that the material in Saturn must be spread out very thinly, making Saturn the least **dense** planet in the Solar System.

The floating planet

Although Saturn is almost as big as Jupiter, Jupiter has far more matter packed into it. In other words, Saturn is less dense. In fact, Saturn is the least dense planet in the Solar System. If you had a large enough bathtub, Saturn would float in it! The low density explains the planet's strange, bulging shape. Because Saturn's gravity is much weaker than Jupiter's, the fast-spinning equatorial regions bulge out further.

Saturn is covered by a hazy layer that masks the cloud bands below. The Hubble Telescope took this false-colour image of Saturn's haze with a camera sensitive to infrared radiation. The haze appears green or yellow, while clearer areas appear blue.

Before the probe hits the cloud tops it falls into a layer of foggy haze. The on-board camera gives you a glimpse of the **rings** arching high overhead, like a glittering white rainbow, before the haze closes in and blurs the view. This hazy layer is much thinner than fog and is almost transparent. And unlike fog, which is made of minute water droplets, the haze is made of tiny crystals of frozen ammonia. The ammonia gives Saturn its creamy colour, masking the natural colours of the cloud bands below.

As the probe sinks deeper, the haze starts to disappear. Then, suddenly, the probe breaks into clear air and you get another surprise. Directly below are Saturn's inner clouds, now revealed in their true colours. Swirling patterns of blue, red, brown and creamy white completely cover the planet, while overhead the Sun shines softly through the semi-transparent haze. The probe analyses Saturn's air and detects **hydrogen** – the same gas that makes up most of the Sun and Jupiter.

The probe releases a parachute to slow down, giving you longer to admire the view. By looking through gaps in the clouds you can make out three layers. The top layer is pale and creamy. Next comes a layer of red and brown clouds, and finally a deeper blue layer. Saturn's clouds, it turns out, are almost exactly the same as Jupiter's

Cloud colours
Saturn's clouds get their colours from the same chemicals as Jupiter's. The top layer of creamy clouds are made of ammonia ice. Next come red and brown clouds of ammonium hydrosulphide, and finally a deep layer of water ice clouds, which mix together with other chemicals to create a blue colour.

What's inside Saturn?

As your probe descends, the pictures it sends back get darker as the **atmosphere** gets thicker. The pressure increases and the air gets steadily hotter. Before long, the signal flickers and dies as the probe is crushed by the hot and choking atmosphere. Even though Saturn is the least **dense** planet, no probe could penetrate all the way to its centre. Astronomers have to figure out what the interior is like from their knowledge of how **hydrogen**, the gas that makes up most of Saturn, acts at high pressures and temperatures.

If you could cut Saturn open and look inside, you would see that the outer cloud layers form just a thin skin around the planet, only 400 kilometres (250 miles) deep.

The planet's interior is a much calmer place than the cloud layers. It is a steadily spinning ball of hydrogen, divided into several distinct shells. Closest to the surface is a thin layer of hydrogen air. This merges gradually into a deep ocean of liquid hydrogen, which also contains **helium**. Towards the bottom of the ocean the hydrogen and helium are compressed and heated by the weight of all the gas and liquid above. As a result, hydrogen **molecules** begin to split apart, forming a sea of individual **atoms**. Astronomers call this form of hydrogen 'metallic' because it behaves like liquid metal. The spinning fluid acts like a giant magnet, generating Saturn's huge **magnetic field**.

In the heart of the planet is a **core** of solid rock, about the size of Earth. If you could stand here, the pressure from overhead would be immense – over a million times Earth's atmospheric pressure – and the temperature would be about 5000°C (9000°F), which is nearly as hot as the surface of the Sun!

hydrogen air

hydrogen and helium ocean

metallic hydrogen

core

Saturn has no real surface. The hydrogen air merges gradually into a hot ocean of liquid hydrogen and helium. The planet's core is a ball of rock the size of Earth.

A day on Saturn

Saturn spins so fast that its day is a mere
ten hours. You can't spend a day on the
surface, so you decide to fly around the
planet to see how day and night affect it.
Sunlight flickers over the ship as you fly
through the **rings'** shadows. The daytime
temperature at the cloud tops is –180°C
(–290°F), but this hardly changes as you
cross to the night side – heat from inside
Saturn keeps the temperature steady.

You notice something odd. In the far south
there are strange colours glowing faintly in
the night sky. You fly closer to investigate.
On the way you pass huge storms that
flash silently with lightning, illuminating
the towering clouds with sudden intensity.

*Saturn's auroras, revealed here by the Hubble Space
Telescope, occur in rings around the poles. Earth has
auroras too, but Saturn's are more spectacular.*

*Lightning is common in Saturn's stormy atmosphere.
The bolts run only from cloud to cloud, unlike the
cloud-to-ground lightning on Earth (above).*

As you approach the **south pole** you
see the cause of the coloured glow: it is
Saturn's **aurora**, or polar lights. Bright
reds, greens and blues dance across the
night sky, forming wavy patterns like
giant curtains. Saturn's aurora is caused
by the **solar wind** – a stream of charged
particles that continually pours out of
the Sun. Particles from the solar wind get
trapped in the planet's magnetic field
and sucked towards the poles, where
they smash into air molecules and release
their energy as light.

Sunrise is approaching, but before the
Sun rises a huge curve of light cuts into
the sky from the dawn horizon. The Sun's
light is spreading across the rings before
it reaches Saturn's atmosphere, and the
icy ring particles are glittering against
the blackness of space.

How Saturn formed

Returning to a higher **orbit,** you wonder how this beautiful and strange planet formed. We know that Saturn and the other **gas giants** were born in very different conditions from those that influenced the birth of Earth and the inner planets, but astronomers are still arguing about precisely what happened.

All the planets in our Solar System formed about 4.5 billion years ago from a huge disk of gas, ice and dust that was left behind after the Sun had formed. The **solar wind** blew most of the gas out of the inner Solar System, and the Sun's heat drove away ice and water. The inner planets formed from the solid materials that were left behind, such as rock and metal.

Further out, however, ice and gases stayed abundant, and these materials formed the outer planets and their moons. There are two theories as to how the gas giants formed. One is that ice and dust **particles** collided and stuck together to form solid **cores** of the outer planets, which then drew in gases through **gravity**. The second theory suggests that the disk of **debris** that surrounded the young Sun broke up into smaller balls of gas and dust, which then contracted to form planets. According to this theory, Saturn's core formed from dust particles that collected in the centre.

This artist's impression shows the Solar System forming from a gigantic cloud of gas and dust that contracted due to gravity. The core of the cloud became the Sun, and most of the remaining material formed the planets.

*The outer planets, such as Saturn and Jupiter (below), formed from different materials than those that make up the inner planets. This artist's impression also shows the **asteroid** belt – a ring of rocky **debris** left over from the Solar System's formation.*

Birth of the rings

With your investigation of Saturn complete, it's time to have another look at the **rings**. This time you fly in an orbit that takes you close to the tops of the main rings. Even from here the rings look solid, so you steer your ship as close as you dare. Now you can see the pieces of ice that make up the rings. These are much larger than the flecks of grit you collected earlier, and range in size from boulders to blocks as big as houses. Yet the rings here are incredibly thin and flat – a mere 10 metres (33 feet) thick. They are kept flat by collisions: any chunk circling Saturn in a tilted orbit would have to pass through the rings, where it would collide with other chunks, reducing the tilt in its orbit.

How did these astonishing rings form? One clue comes from Saturn's gravity. The rings lie in an area where the planet's gravity would tear apart any large object in orbit, and prevent debris from clumping together to form a moon. So are the rings debris left over from Saturn's formation? Astronomers doubt this because of the vast amount of material present. If Saturn had always had rings, most of the material would by now have fallen into the planet, and there would be little left in orbit. Saturn's rings must therefore have formed recently. A likely explanation is that the rings are the remains of an icy moon that was smashed to pieces by a collision with a **comet**. Small moons within the rings probably help to replenish the material with pieces of ice chipped from their surfaces

Comet Hyakutake blazes across the sky in this photograph. Comets are huge balls of dirty ice. A cataclysmic collision between a moon and comet may have given birth to Saturn's rings.

The Saturn System

It's time to investigate Saturn's moons, so you steer your ship away from the **rings**. Saturn has a large family of at least eighteen moons. These range from small, uneven rocks a few kilometres across to huge Titan, which is larger than the planets Mercury and Pluto and has an **atmosphere** of its own.

Closest to Saturn, **orbiting** within or very close to the rings, are the so-called shepherd moons. Astronomers have named six shepherd moons so far: Pan, Atlas, Prometheus, Pandora, Epimetheus and Janus. These moons are thought to influence the structure of the rings, and there may be many more of them. The largest are around 160 kilometres (100 miles) across.

Saturn and its moons are like a miniature version of the Solar System. This artist's impression shows most of the large moons, seen from Hyperion. In order from Saturn they are Mimas, Enceladus, Tethys, Dione, Rhea and Titan (not to scale).

Saturn

Prometheus Janus Mimas

Telesto
Calypso   Helene

Pan   Atlas

Pandora Epimetheus   Enceladus

Tethys   Dione

Rhea

Hyperion

Phoebe

Iapetus

Titan

Beyond Saturn's rings are larger moons. These seem to come in pairs: Mimas and Enceladus are 400–500 kilometres (250–300 miles) across, while farther out Tethys and Dione are both around 1100 kilometres (700 miles) across. Tethys and Dione share their orbits with smaller moons – Telesto and Calypso and Helene. All these worlds orbit closer to Saturn than our Moon does to Earth.

Saturn's eighteen moons are shown here to scale, except for Pan, Atlas, Telesto, Calypso and Helene, which have been multiplied in size by five. Order from the left shows the order from Saturn.

Farther out the system gets slightly less crowded. Rhea, 1500 kilometres (940 miles) across, is next, and then giant Titan, 5000 kilometres (3000 miles) wide and 1.2 million kilometres (750,000 miles) away from Saturn. Beyond Titan is tiny Hyperion, then Iapetus, a strange moon roughly the size of Rhea and 3.6 million kilometres (2.2 million miles) from Saturn. The last and most distant moon, Phoebe, is just 220 kilometres (140 miles) across, and is probably an **asteroid** captured by Saturn's **gravity** – it orbits in the opposite direction to all the other moons, in a stretched orbit that takes it up to 12 million kilometres (7.5 million miles) from the planet.

Where did all these moons come from? Astronomers think they formed from material left behind after Saturn was born, in the same way that the planets formed from the Sun's leftovers. The pattern of moons around Saturn mimics the layout of the Solar System, with the large worlds in the middle, and small ones close in or far out. One mystery, though, is why Saturn has only one giant moon, while Jupiter has four. Perhaps the answer lies in the fact that the Jupiter system formed from a much larger **mass** of material than the Saturn system.

Gian Domenico Cassini (1625–1712)

The Italian-born French astronomer Cassini was one of the greatest astronomers of his time. As well as discovering the Cassini division in Saturn's rings, he discovered four of Saturn's moons.

Shepherd moons

The shepherd moons are misshapen lumps of ice just a few kilometres across. Astronomers are not sure how they formed. They may have formed at the same time as the other moons, but were too close to Saturn to combine into a larger world. Or they may be the remains of a large moon that was smashed by a **comet** or torn apart by Saturn's **gravity**.

Because the shepherds are close to Saturn, they run the risk of being struck by any comets, **asteroids** or **meteorites** pulled in by the planet's gravity. They are probably hit fairly often, and small chunks of ice are constantly being chipped off them, adding to Saturn's **rings**.

ABOVE: *The shepherd moon Pandora is named after a woman from Greek mythology. When Pandora opened her magical box, evil spread into the world.*

The shepherd moons have just enough gravity to sweep up stray material from within the rings, creating distinct gaps between the individual rings. In this way, they 'shepherd' the ring material – hence their name. Their gravity might also create the short-lived, spoke-like gaps that run across the rings in some places.

The moon Pan is named after the Greek god of shepherds. According to mythology, Pan had a human body but the legs, ears and horns of a goat.

Mimas

After flying past the shepherd moons you head for Mimas, a brilliant white world pockmarked with thousands of craters. The largest of these, called Herschel, is more than 130 kilometres (80 miles) across – nearly a third as wide as the moon itself. Over millions of years, Saturn's gravity has pulled Mimas this way and that, gradually slowing down the moon's **rotation** so that it now spins once in every orbit around Saturn. As a result, one side of Mimas permanently faces its parent planet, while the other side never sees it.

The Herschel Crater on Mimas is so big that you can see it from thousands of kilometres away.

You land close to the centre of the Herschel Crater and step out onto the airless surface. The ground is covered with powdery ice, and you have to wear studded boots to keep a grip in the very weak **gravity.** A quick test shows that the ice is nearly pure water – Mimas is a giant iceball!

In the distance you can see the huge wall of mountains that forms the crater rim, but your view is dominated by Herschel's central mountains – peaks of solid ice 4 kilometres (2.5 miles) high. Herschel is an **impact crater**, formed by collision with a comet or asteroid millions of years ago. The central mountains formed when the ground bounced back after the impact. Behind you, Saturn hangs motionless on the horizon. From Mimas you get a spectacular view of the rings, which appear paper thin because you see them edge-on. The planet itself looks like a giant golden dome, with hundreds of black lines etched into it where the rings have cast shadows.

Towering ice mountains rise from the middle of the crater floor in this artist's impression of the Herschel Crater.

Enceladus

*ABOVE: From the surface of Enceladus you can see the vast **crescent** of Saturn perched on the horizon, as in this artist's impression. Saturn's **rings** form a sharp line across its middle. If you shield your eyes, you can see the fainter outlying ring, within which Enceladus orbits.*

As you approach Enceladus, you start to see surprising details: there is only a light scattering of craters, large flat open plains and long ridges. The land looks as though it has been covered over in the recent past, wiping out many **impact craters**. In some areas, the surface is so new that it hasn't had time to become cratered.

You land on Enceladus and step out on to a crunchy surface covered in frost. Stooping down, you scoop up a handful and roll it into a ball – it is surprisingly soft, like newly fallen snow. You throw the ball high into the air and it disappears into the sky, turning over and over and catching the distant sunlight. **Gravity** here is so weak that the snowball will not fall for hours.

The icy ground is covered by parallel grooves that stretch to the horizon. Enceladus is so small that the horizon is noticeably curved, and it looks much closer than on Earth.

Brightest moon

Enceladus is 500 kilometres (310 miles) wide and orbits 178,000 kilometres (110,000 miles) above Saturn's cloud tops, circling it in less than 33 hours. Of all the moons in the Solar System, icy Enceladus has the brightest surface.

Suddenly you feel the ground tremble. A large mound of snow lies a short distance away, and, as you watch, a cloud of gas bursts out of it, shooting up into the sky before sputtering out. The gas is water vapour, which forms ice crystals in the coldness of space. A short while later, some of the crystals fall back to the surface as snow.

You're puzzled, though: small moons like Enceladus are generally inactive, heavily cratered worlds, like nearby Mimas. Why is this one different? The most likely explanation is that the interior of Enceladus is heated up by a gravitational tug of war between Saturn and its moons, mainly Tethys and Dione. Enceladus's **orbit** is noticeably stretched, and the forces acting on it are constantly changing. Every so often, the moon might even get warm enough for large parts of its surface to melt and re-form, creating the ridges and valleys that mark the flat plains. This process is called **tidal heating.**

*ABOVE: An ice **geyser** erupts. Astronomers think that such features are continuously recarpeting the surface of Enceladus, accounting for the lack of craters in many places. Since gravity is so low, one eruption could easily cover the whole moon in snow. Ice from a geyser blown far out into space might also be the source of Saturn's faint outer ring.*

The icy moons

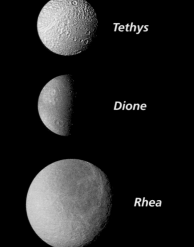

Tethys

Dione

Rhea

Leaving Enceladus behind, you make a quick tour of some other midsize moons: first Tethys, then Dione and finally Rhea. Unlike Titan, these moons are not large enough to hold on to an **atmosphere**. Their bright, reflective surfaces show that they are made from rock and ice, just like Enceladus. You notice that all three moons have surface gashes and signs of ancient ice eruptions.

Unlike Enceladus, these moons have not experienced **tidal heating**. Heat generated by **radioactive chemicals** might have warmed up their interiors enough to melt the ice. On Tethys and Dione, this ice erupted onto the surface through vents such as **geysers**, covering up many craters.

One mystery is why Rhea, the second largest of Saturn's moons, is covered in thousands of craters and shows few signs of this past activity. The best theory is that Rhea's **mass** worked against it: as the moon cooled and its slushy interior began to freeze, pressure from Rhea's outer layers produced a **dense** ice called ice-2. Since ice-2 takes up less space than normal ice, Rhea shrank, tightly sealing any ice geysers and volcanoes in the process.

BELOW: On Tethys you make sure to visit the Ithaca Chasma, a must-see on any trip to the Saturn system. This huge trench stretches almost from pole to pole. In this artist's impression the 100-kilometre- (60-mile-) wide canyon lies before you. In some places it is up to five kilometres (three miles) deep.

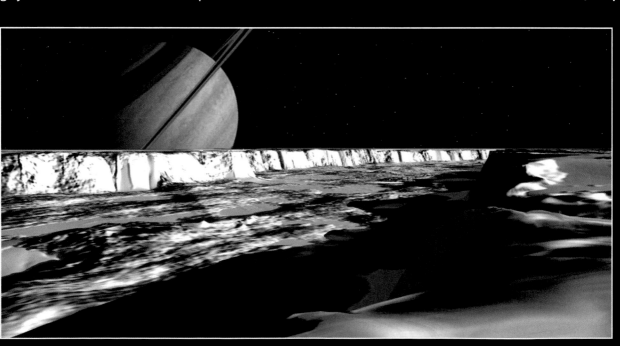

ABOVE: This artist's impression shows strange land formations inside a crater on Dione. The surface of Dione, like that of Tethys, is not heavily cratered all over – ancient ice eruptions have smoothed parts of it over.

*BELOW: On pockmarked Rhea, you visit two of the largest craters: Izanagi ('the larger') and Izanami ('the smaller'). The craters overlap, so you see both at the same time, as in this artist's impression. While you take in the view, a small **meteorite** strikes Izanagi. The ridges and huge cliffs that you can see were probably formed when Rhea shrank.*

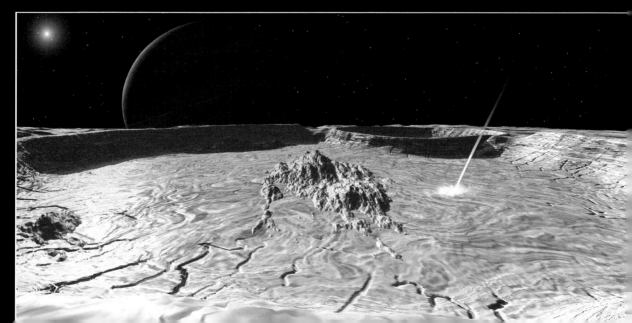

Titan

Titan is a disappointment at first. As you go into **orbit** around the moon, you can see no surface detail – just a featureless orange ball. Titan's air is orange because it contains a gas called methane. The murky air completely covers the moon, but your instruments show there is solid land below. This means you can land on Titan to explore.

After a careful touchdown, you put on your spacesuit and step outside. The orange sky is very hazy, but you can see Saturn shining dimly through it, dominating the horizon. Your instruments show that the air is mostly nitrogen – the same gas that makes up most of Earth's air. Methane makes up only a few per cent of the total.

The landscape around you is orangey brown and the ground is wet and slippery. It's raining, but the rain can't possibly be water. Titan's surface is extremely cold – about –180°C (–290°F) – so water would fall as snow, not rain. You collect some of the mysterious liquid to analyse. It's thick and greasy like oil, and it turns out to be an **organic chemical** called ethane. Ethane is highly **flammable** on Earth, but there's no oxygen here so nothing can burn. Otherwise one spark could set fire to the whole moon!

Seen from space, Titan is a smooth orange globe.

You make your way toward the summit of a nearby hill. Even though you weigh only a third of your Earth weight in Titan's low **gravity**, walking is difficult. It's a bit like being caught in an oil slick, squelching through oily puddles that suck at your boots. Eventually you reach the summit and find yourself at the top of a cliff, with a spectacular view across a lake of ethane. The rain has washed the rocky ground clear at your feet, so you stoop down to chip away a rock sample to take back to the ship.

Once back on board and out of your sticky spacesuit, you analyse the sample. It turns out to be the same mixture of rock and ice that makes up Saturn's other large moons. But why is Titan's surface so different?

Astronomers think the interior of Titan got very hot and melted during the large moon's formation. In contrast, Saturn's other, smaller moons cooled down, because small objects tend to lose heat quickly. Titan's hot interior caused gases to bubble out of the surface, forming the thick **atmosphere** and oily rain. Billions of years ago Earth had a similar atmosphere, but our atmosphere was gradually transformed by the action of living organisms. Titan is too cold for liquid water, so life cannot exist here. As a result, its atmosphere has stayed unchanged, like a fossil version of the primitive Earth.

*The background picture is an artist's impression of the surface of Titan, with a small **space probe** parachuting down over an ethane lake. NASA is planning to drop a probe onto Titan in 2004.*

Christiaan Huygens
(1629–1693)
The Dutch astronomer and instrument-maker Christiaan Huygens made several important scientific discoveries and inventions, including the pendulum clock. After learning how to grind lenses for telescopes, he built the finest instruments of the age and used them to study the rings of Saturn. In the winter of 1655 he discovered Titan. Other astronomers, including English architect Sir Christopher Wren (1632–1723), had seen Titan before but had mistaken it for a star.

Iapetus and Phoebe

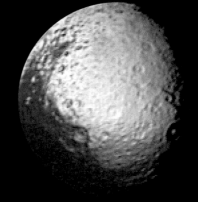

Saturn's outermost two moons are very strange. When Iapetus was first discovered, astronomers could see it when it was on one side of Saturn but not when it was on the other. The only explanation was that Iapetus must have a bright half and a very dark half. As you fly past the large moon you can see for yourself that the theory is correct – it's as if one side of Iapetus has been painted black, while the other side is almost white.

Like the other moons, Iapetus keeps one face permanently locked towards Saturn. As a result, Iapetus has a **leading side**, which faces forwards as the moon travels through space, and a **trailing side**, which faces backwards. The leading side is the dark part of Iapetus, while the trailing side is as bright and icy as Saturn's other moons. The side of Iapetus that faces Saturn is half light and half dark.

ABOVE: *The dark and bright parts of Iapetus show up clearly in this photograph from the* Voyager 2 *space probe.*

BELOW: *The dark side of Iapetus is a land of hills, mountains and strange, wavy ice formations, as shown in this artist's impression.*

At the boundary between the two faces, dark and light landscapes mingle – craters on the dark side have bright, icy bottoms, while mountains on the light side have picked up dark coatings where they face into the moon's **orbit**. It looks as if Iapetus is actually an icy moon that has picked up a dark coating by flying into a cloud of soot.

Where could this sooty material have come from? One possible answer emerges as you get close to Phoebe. This moon must be an intruder in the Saturn system because it's orbiting the planet in the wrong direction. Phoebe is probably a captured **asteroid**. Its surface is not icy white, but dark and sooty like the leading side of Iapetus.

Phoebe is only 115 kilometres (70 miles) wide. It is just large enough to have pulled itself into a ball shape under its own **gravity**, but it is not a perfect sphere. The surface is heavily cratered, and you can see deep **crevasses** gouged into it. It has obviously had a violent past – perhaps it was torn apart and reassembled as it was captured and pulled into orbit around Saturn.

It seems that dust from Phoebe's dark surface has coated Iapetus, but how did it get there? One theory is that it is being blasted off the surface of Phoebe by tiny **meteorites**. As Saturn's gravity pulls the dark dust inward, it eventually crosses the orbit of Iapetus, and the inner moon sweeps it up.

Saturn appears small from Phoebe, the outermost moon. This artist's impression shows the view from the bottom of a deep crevasse.

Early observations

Saturn was named after a Roman harvest god whose festival was celebrated in midwinter. Although the planet has been seen since the earliest times, little was known about it until the invention of the telescope around 1608.

Because Saturn is so far away, it was difficult to see clearly with early telescopes. But Italian astronomer Galileo Galilei (1564–1642) still noticed that there was something strange about the planet's shape. He suggested it might be a triple planet, while others suggested that Saturn might have handles. The astronomers had seen Saturn's **rings**, but they didn't yet know what they were. A few years later the rings disappeared, adding to the mystery.

Dutch astronomer Christiaan Huygens (1629–1693) finally solved the mystery around 1655, and his ring theory was soon proved right when others observed the shadow the rings cast onto Saturn. Shortly after, Gian Domenico Cassini (1625–1712) discovered the division in the rings that now bears his name. Huygens and Cassini also found the first of Saturn's moons – Huygens recorded Titan, while Cassini found Iapetus, Rhea, Tethys and Dione.

ABOVE: *Italian astronomer Galileo Galilei was the first to notice Saturn's strange, lumpy shape while observing it through a telescope. We now know that its peculiar shape is due to its rings.*

BELOW: *The Paris Observatory, built 1667–1672, is where Cassini discovered four of Saturn's moons and the division in the planet's rings that is named after him.*

Huygens and Cassini discovered all these moons at times when the rings were edge-on, and so the moons were not lost in their glare. Even today astronomers look for new moons at these times.

Saturn's family of moons grew as astronomers discovered more, but the planet itself remained a mystery. Although telescopes were getting more powerful, it was another century before William Herschel (1738–1822) saw the first markings on Saturn's surface, and used the movement of a white spot (actually an enormous storm) to calculate the length of Saturn's day. By the 20th century, astronomers were regularly recording bands and spots on Saturn, including a 30-year cycle of storms in the northern **hemisphere**. They also realized that Saturn, like Jupiter, was a giant ball of gas.

Saturn's rings were another mystery. At first astronomers had thought they were solid, although Cassini had suggested they might be made up of thousands of tiny moons. In the 1850s James Clerk Maxwell backed up Cassini's theory with mathematics. But it was not until 1895 that astrophysicist James Edward Keeler, from the USA, used light from the rings to show that different segments were **rotating** at different speeds, and so Cassini and Maxwell had to be right.

ABOVE: *The German-born British astronomer William Herschel discovered two of Saturn's moons – Mimas and Enceladus – as well as calculating the length of the planet's day.*

James Clerk Maxwell
(1831–1879)
*The British physicist James Clerk Maxwell is most famous for his theory that light travels in waves as a form of energy known as **electromagnetism**. This electromagnetic theory laid the foundations for Einstein's theory of relativity. Maxwell also investigated the properties of gases, and this led to his interest in Saturn's rings. He used his knowledge of how materials behave to show that a solid or liquid ring in **orbit** around Saturn would inevitably break apart, and that only a swarm of small chunks of material could remain in stable orbit for a long time.*

Probes to Saturn

Because Saturn is so far out in the Solar System, it takes many years for even a high-speed **space probe** to reach it. But the three that have travelled there so far have transformed astronomers' ideas about the planet and revealed many of its secrets.

The Voyager probes were the first to photograph the major moons of Saturn. This artist's impression shows the main dish used to beam pictures back to Earth.

BELOW: *This artist's impression shows the* Huygens *probe (right) and its parachute after a successful landing on the surface of Titan.* Huygens *is scheduled to land on Titan in November 2004.*

The first probe to Saturn, *Pioneer 11*, was launched in April 1973 on a joint **mission** to Jupiter and Saturn. When *Pioneer* flew past Jupiter in December 1974 it used the planet's **gravity** to catapult it towards Saturn at a higher speed. Even so, it did not reach Saturn until September 1979. *Pioneer* was primitive by today's standards, but it returned the first close-up images of the planet, revealed the detailed structure of the **rings**, and detected Saturn's **radiation** and **magnetic fields.**

Pioneer also provided information that helped astronomers plan the next missions to Saturn. Although they were launched only four years later, *Voyagers 1* and *2* were far more advanced than *Pioneer*. These probes took a grand tour of the outer Solar System by taking advantage of a special alignment of the planets that happens once every 175 years. *Voyager 1* visited Jupiter and Saturn, while *Voyager 2* visited both these planets before continuing on to Uranus and Neptune. Both Voyagers made important discoveries at Saturn. They photographed the major moons for the first time, found several new moons, and they discovered faint outer and inner rings outside the zone of Saturn's main rings.

An ambitious new space probe to Saturn is expected to arrive at the planet in 2004. The *Cassini* probe will be the first to go into orbit around the planet, rather than flying quickly past as earlier probes did.

Cassini left Earth in 1997. In order to pick up enough speed to reach Saturn, the probe is taking a complex, looping path across the Solar System. First it flies past Venus twice, then Earth, and then past Jupiter. Each planet gives it an extra boost of speed. When *Cassini* arrives at Saturn it will spend several years surveying the planet, its rings and its large family of moons.

The most exciting part of *Cassini*'s mission is the plan to drop a smaller probe onto the mysterious moon Titan. The *Huygens* probe will plunge through Titan's thick **atmosphere** and then parachute gently to the ground – unless it lands in a sea. As it floats down, *Huygens* will analyse the chemicals in Titan's air and take hundreds of pictures of the landscape below. If *Huygens* reaches the ground, it may even be able to study the chemicals there and take more pictures. The combined efforts of *Cassini* and *Huygens* should tell us a great deal more about Saturn and its moons.

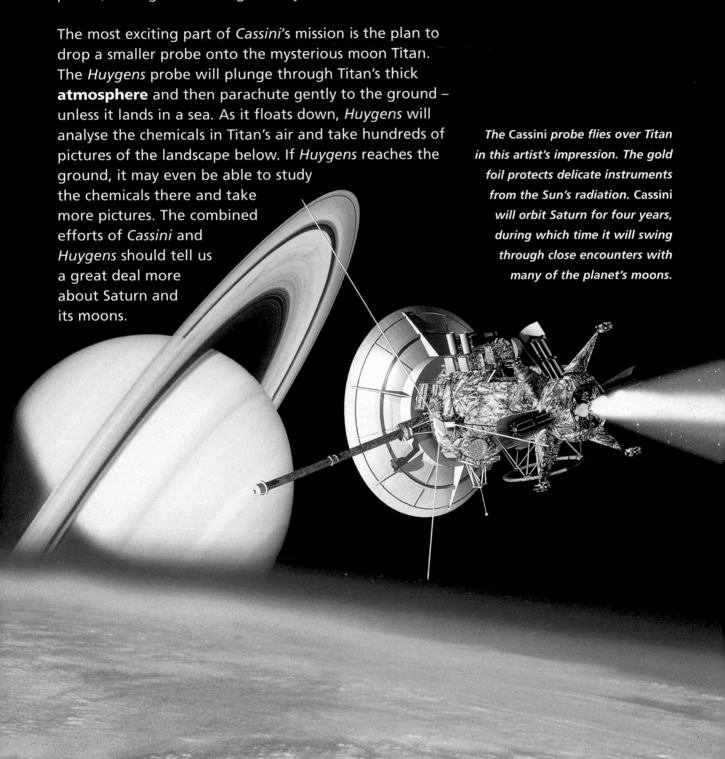

The Cassini *probe flies over Titan in this artist's impression. The gold foil protects delicate instruments from the Sun's radiation.* Cassini *will orbit Saturn for four years, during which time it will swing through close encounters with many of the planet's moons.*

A crewed expedition to Saturn is unlikely to happen in our lifetimes, unless faster rockets are invented, or scientists find out how to put astronauts into suspended animation. Saturn itself has no solid surface on which to build a base, so astronauts would have to choose a moon to settle on. All the moons are bitterly cold, with temperatures around −130°C (−200°F). Sunlight is so feeble in the Saturn system that solar power would be useless, and some other sort of fuel would be needed.

Titan might seem a promising place for a base. The **organic chemicals** on Titan could be used as fuel or to make a range of other substances, and any ice trapped below the moon's surface could be used as a water supply, or as a source of oxygen to make breathable air. But Titan might be too dangerous. If oxygen was released into the **atmosphere**, the organic chemicals might catch fire and turn the planet into a blazing inferno. Perhaps astronauts would find it safer to build an airtight base on one of the nearby icy moons, such as Hyperion, and make occasional trips to Titan to collect valuable materials.

If humans ever visit the Saturn system, perhaps they would set up a base on one of the icy moons, such as Hyperion, shown here in an artist's impression.

Glossary

asteroid large chunk of rock left over from when the planets formed

atmosphere layer of gas trapped by gravity around the surface of a planet

atom minute particle of matter

aurora colourful glow in the sky caused by charged particles hitting the atmosphere

axis imaginary line through the middle of a planet or moon that it spins around

comet large chunk of ice left over from when the planets formed. Comets grow long, glowing tails when near the Sun.

core centre of a planet or moon

crescent curved shape like one segment of an orange

crevasse huge crack in icy ground, forming a narrow trench between tall cliffs

debris fragments of rock, dust, ice or other materials floating in space

dense having a lot of mass squeezed into a small space

equator imaginary line around the middle of a planet, moon or star

flammable able to burn

gas giant huge planet made out of gas. Jupiter and Saturn are gas giants.

geyser eruption of water and steam from underground

gravity force that pulls objects together. The heavier or closer an object is, the stronger its gravity, or pull.

helium chemical found in the atmosphere of Saturn and Jupiter

hemisphere top or bottom half of a planet, moon or star

hydrogen simplest, lightest and most common element in the Universe. Hydrogen makes up most of the gas in the Sun and in the planets Jupiter and Saturn.

impact crater circular crater made when a comet, asteroid or meteorite smashes into a planet or moon

infrared radiation invisible rays of heat that travel at the speed of light

leading side side of a planet that faces into the direction of travel

magnetic field region around a planet, moon or star where a compass can detect the north pole

mass measure of the amount of matter in an object. Mass is similar to weight, but objects only have weight when they are on a planet.

meteor small piece of space rock that burns up in a planet's atmosphere, producing a streak of light called a shooting star

meteorite space rock that lands on the surface of a planet or moon

mission expedition to visit or observe a specific target in space, such as a planet

molecule tiny unit of matter consisting of two or more atoms joined together

north pole point on the surface of a planet, moon or star that coincides with the top end of its axis

orbit path an object takes around another when it is trapped by the larger object's gravity; or, to take such a path

organic chemical chemical made up of molecules containing carbon atoms

particle tiny fragment of an atom. Particle can also mean a speck of dust or dirt.

pole point on the surface of a planet, moon or star that coincides with the top or bottom end of its axis

radiation energy released in rays from a source. Heat and light are types of radiation.

radioactive chemical unstable chemical that emits dangerous types of radiation

ring circle made up of millions of ice or rock particles orbiting together around a planet

rotation movement of a planet, moon or star turning around its centre, or axis

solar wind constant stream of particles that travel out of the Sun and through the solar system at very high speed

south pole point on the surface of a planet, moon or star that coincides with the bottom end of its axis

space probe robotic vehicle sent from Earth to study the solar system

spacewalk walk outside a spaceship while the ship is in space

tidal heating heating of a moon's interior as it is pulled in different directions by the gravity of its parent planet and other moons

trailing side side of a planet that faces away from the direction of travel

Books and websites

Couper, Heather and Henbest, Nigel. *The DK Space Encyclopedia*. London: Dorling Kindersley, 1999.

Furniss, Tim. *The Solar System – Spinning Through Space*. London: Hodder Wayland (Hodder & Stoughton Children's Division), 1999.

Kerrod, Robin. *Our Solar System – Giant Planets*. London: Belitha Press Ltd, 2000.

nssdc.gsfc.nasa.gov/photo_gallery/ – NASA NSSDC Photo Gallery

pds.jpl.nasa.gov/planets/welcome/saturn.htm – NASA Profile

seds.lpl.arizona.edu/nineplanets/nineplanets/saturn.html – Nine Planets (Saturn)

www.discovery.com/area/science/cassini/cassini1.html – Cassini Sailing to Saturn

www.jpl.nasa.gov/cassini/Kids – NASA Cassini

Index

Picture Credits
Key: t – top, b – below, c – centre, l – left, r – right. **NASA**: 3, 4–5b, 7r, 8b, 9t, 9b, 10t, 12, 13t, 13b, 23t, 25t, 26tr, 26cr, 26br, 28t, 30t, Ames Research Center 14t, ESA/D. Ducros 34b, JPL/California Institute of Technology 2, 11, 21t, 23b, 24–25, 26b, 27t, 27b, 28–29, 30b, 31, 34t, 36, Erich Karkoschka/University of Arizona 10b, 15t, J.T. Trauger/JPL 17t; **SOHO***: 4l; **Hulton Getty**: 21b; **Mary Evans Picture Library**: 22b, Edwin Wallace 22t; **Science Photo Library**: 1, 20, 29, 32t, 32b, 33b, Dennis Di Cicco/Peter Arnold Inc 8tl, David Ducros 35, David A. Hardy 18t, Keith Kent 17b, Jerry Lodriguss 19, Sheila Terry 33t, Detlev Van Ravenswaay 18b. Front Cover: NASA. Back Cover: NASA, JPL/California Institute of Technology.
*SOHO is a project of international cooperation between ESA & NASA.